A POETIC JOURNEY

Naomi Matthews
And
Jake Mitchell

TABLE OF CONTENTS

DEDICATION

I would like to dedicate my first project "A Poetic Journey" to my siblings; Talethia, Ralethia, Jake, Esau, Florine, A'korie, O'korie, Margie, and James. No one understands the heart of my pain and triumph like you all. I love you dearly; each one of us has a story to tell and a testimony, continue to shine bright.

I also dedicate this book and so much more to my children, Monteze Matthews and Jabrone Dubose.

Sisters are Forever

My five sisters are the shit, let's start with my big sister Kesha, you see Kesha is this fierce lioness type of sista the kind you look up to you know what I mean , Kesha also can hook some hair up like nobody's business that's my sista. Next up is my ride or die chick Ms. Ree Ree, my always got my back, been there since day one sista, Ms. Diva in the flesh Ralethia. Next up is my sweet soft spoken little sister Florine, Florine has always been my baby and I adore her sweet spirit and loving heart always and forever. Next up is my baby sister The Poetic Hooper Margie, my girl exudes strength and she don't play about her family. Last but not least is my sister from another mother my right hand girl the one who keeps me lifted the one and only Shakelia Vontrice. I love my beautiful talented and oh so fierce sisters.

ACKNOWLEGMENTS

Thank you Jake Mitchell for taking this Journey with me, you are a great poet and a phenomenal writer, I wish you nothing but the best on your journey to success.

Thank you Flenardo Taylor for all the advice and guidance along the way, I really appreciate your drive and whether you've noticed or not I am definitely watching and learning from you.

Thank you Yolanda Latimore for Poetic Peace Arts, having that type of platform in Macon, Georgia has allowed me to open up and grow in my craft.

Thank you to Team Hungry, Plus Effect, Enigmatic Mahogany, and other Internet Radio shows that allow Poets and Artist to display their talents weekly, I am very thankful for this platform for allowing me to express myself through poetry.

Thank you to all of my supporters, without you this would have remained a dream.

Thank you to my lovely mother Teresa Mitchell for blessing me with such a marvelous gift to you I am eternally indebted.

Thank to my number one fan Taiesha Penniman for supporting my dream!

The Love That Missed Me

I miss the way he kisses, but its funny his kiss missed me.

I miss the way he hugs, but it is strange his hugs missed me.

I miss the way he touches, but its weird his touch missed me.

I miss the way he loves, but it is odd his love missed me.

Could it be that I imagined the sweetest kiss

Could it be that I imagined the tightest hug or

Could it be that I imagined the warmest touch

Is it possible that I imagined the deepest love?

Only a fool would imagine a love so distant, yet I remember every instant

A hopeless romantic is what society would have predicted

I just thank God, I missed it…

My Man

I love the way my man enlightens me with his wise words and Mature mind, he allows me to learn from him, his experience stimulates me completely. My man can be Arrogant, but I guess that something that make him so desirable, because I too can be a handful. My man is so Radiant, his presence brightens up my spirits, he has a glow that ignites a fire deep within. My Man is Tough, so masculine, but touches me so gently. He makes me feel so secure when we are together as if we just cannot be touched. My man is Intelligent, his intellect is unique, he shares his knowledge with me and I receive all that he has to offer. My man is Noble, he always does what is right, he is a man that I am proud to say is mine. I love the way he loves me and always gives his all I love my man!

COEXIST

There are moments in our lives that we come to the realization that the plans of our hearts and the plans of her minds cannot coexist. We all fantasize about the sweetest kiss or loves bliss. We feel our hearts beating to a special type of drum. Heartache and pain that we think we will never overcome somehow fades away like the moon when it meets the sun. The problem that illuminates without any disguise seems to be the past that intertwines with a sudden future filled with hope, but now is bombarded with insecurities and fears threatening the very happiness of love's will. Yesterday's heartache and pain rains down as though it had been deeply missed. This is a sign that we internalize as we once again conclude that the plans of our hearts and the plans of or minds simply cannot coexist.

UNKNOWN LOVE

Free spirit, loving, kind, sweet these attributes I use to describe myself. I am in love with love a hopeless romantic some may say, yearning for something I never had. Only mere glimpses in my dreams, I often wish for things that were unseen in my world, a world that was once filled with heartache and despair now flows a river of optimism. The sweet fragrance and the soft touch of an unknown love linger in my heart and there it will remain under lock and key until that day when all my fears and all my past along with my wall will come tumbling down and my unknown love will forever be found.

My Passion

Poetry is my passion my very heartbeat. My thoughts and feelings come together on a steady beat. Words so deep they pierce your mind and leave your soul weak. Not weak like a being that lacks energy, but weak because your mental lacks substance. So I offer you up this food I will feed you lyrically. The more you hear the more you begin to crave. Stories about how my heart was broken, how I was abused, and how I made it out unscathed. This opens a pathway into who I am all the good the bad and the ugly not just the glitz and glam. My words are expressions and with these words, I connect with who I am, who I was, and who I will be. Poetry to me is an obsession it gives me life. This art form is apart of me and until forever will remain my destiny.

I was Young Once

I once knew a man whose friendship was absolutely Tempting

This man's presence was Intense

His love was utterly Mind blowing

To allow him in was Overwhelming

However, his touch was Tender

With him, I explored new Heights

Our love was Young

Yet every moment was Outstanding

His virtuous demeanor was Unique

Although our hopes of holding on were Naive

His subtle entry into my life was Grand

God's Grace

Let us take a moment to talk about how God's grace saved my life.

Depression consumed me.

I crept down hell's alley and thought its embrace would take my pain away.

I grew up in Satan's arms and oh to often would go astray.

Yearning for acceptance, I accepted whatever the world would throw my way.

I stared death in its face and welcomed it with open arms.

All because I fell in love sin, and was mesmerized by her undeniable charm.

But who knew God had a plan for me?

I recall it like it was yesterday the moment when I reached out for his unchanging hand.

I asked God to restore me; suddenly I began to trust more in him and less in man.

This was during a time when I was emerged in an unholy yet intense love affair.

Until God spared my life I viewed the world and I as a perfect pair.

Now that I surrender to his will, I cannot deny his love

And that's the story about how God's amazing grace saved my life.

Happy Pill

All of these thoughts floating around in my head anxious nights I lay awake in bed with hands sweaty heart pounding, it's astounding how in a blink of an eye my entire mood changes.

And what's strange is even though I know it is a temporary surge of emotions I began to digest this happy pill in hopes that it will help with my coping. You see ever since I was a baby girl born into this wicked world I've faced adversities. With the most important people in my life hurting me starting with my mother deserting me when I was only 6 months old, where was my happy pill then?

Or how about when my own kin who took away my innocence. I can remember back then coping in a sense, I fed on attention. As I grew older, my abused heart grew colder with every attempt to mend it. Depression nearly killed me, so some random doctor offered me something that would heal me, but I was refusing because in my head I didn't want to begin using.

I didn't need a drug to erase my pain besides; if I take them they would label me insane, but wait Rewind 9 years later I've become 10 times greater because I took every negative turned it into a positive mixed with a hint of my Happy Pill and I'm still here.

The Affair

The words he spoke sunk into the frontal lobe of my brain shooting stimulating pain to my heart. I began to sit back and reflect on those moments when I felt pure and utter neglect. Could it be I fell victim to my own insecurities or is it true he plotted to allure me into his web? Now I'm regretting how easily I invited this man into my bed. He has explored the most intimate parts to me that only the man who wants my hand should seek. Will this occur every time I allow him to peek inside my mind? Has the intertwining of our paths so effortlessly been defined by just one night? It is true I should no better but with every thought of his touch I became wetter, and the will to fight that urge became heavier and heavier. So who is to blame, is it him for taking aim at my awkward loneliness or I for rocking that little pink sundress? I knew exactly what I was doing, the need to fill that empty void I was pursuing. Now the story has been written but the desires I feel must remain hidden.

Claim Me…

Damn you're heavy on my brain keeping my composure is hard to maintain thinking about 10/25 is driving me insane trying fight off these urges to scream out your name after that night, b.o.b's no longer the same. Touching myself trying to refrain, reminiscing about the first, second, third time that I came. On 10/26 pleasing you was my aim, making love with my mouth, stepping up my head game. Could you tell from my moans I enjoy pleasurable pain? Now I'm confused about my emotions because I'm feeling ashamed. I appear to be a freak that hasn't been tamed, but I can show you I'm a good girl that wants to be changed. So it's not just my body, but my soul that I want you to claim.

Free Spirit

I love being the weird girl; it is something about me that exudes quirkiness to the 10th degree, so full of life and free to explore the world through a lens of creativity. My inner most desires spills out as I began to speak. I dream big, bigger than the tallest mountain or deepest ocean. I dare to be unlike any other, never fitting perfectly inside a box made to conform me. I love the very idea of love itself and its radiant light beams from my soul. A luminous smile as bright as a million suns finds itself parading across my face on any giving day. I stand out like a sore thumb and I love every bit of me. I am free to know myself on different levels and embrace the uniqueness of me. My free spirit is the first thing people see when they walk near me. It's because I walk with a bit of a switch and I appear as though my life is glitch free. Carefree loving me, the world, and everything in it, because from the beginning I had this twinkle in my eye that told a story about a bold young girl destine to take this world by storm… And I did!

Room Full of People

I find it funny how in a room full of people I often feel as though I am the only person who exists. So far from reality or out of place, I desperately try to remember where I'm going but never forget where I came from. As I look back on my past, at times it is a struggle not to fall back into the same thinking traps that once consumed me. When you look at me you see this smile but you don't know the pain that once hid behind it, but I hope you see the joy that now shines through it. Yeah I have my days when I feel like I'm alone in a room full of people, but as long as those days when I feel like I'm on top of the world and the world is the best place ever out way those lonely days I know I'll be ok!

Lost Dreams

I have to get a hold of my emotions because I'm so sick of men placing their tainted fingerprints on my heart every time I reach out my hand to greet them with a subtle hello. Once the introduction has faded away, I am left with broken memories that linger. Now I have more baggage to pile on top of this heap I so eagerly attempted hide behind this bright smile. I anxiously count the moments praying the next one is courteous enough to leave a piece of my soul behind. Now I am avoiding questions like, why do you so easily offer up my gift and can we just be friends? If only I could find a way to get a hold of these emotions I could greet a man with a subtle hello without the long nights filled with lost dreams and me tossing and turning throughout the night. These lost dreams are frightening, heart tightening each time I watch you walk away. You, the same you that promised me the world. You said I will never leave you reminiscing, but oddly, something's missing… You!

PRETENDERS

I can't stand people persistently prying open prehistoric wounds portraying that they care

bout me.

Reminiscing on random negative renditions of yesteryear.

With envious eyes they're quick to tell lies, enemies in disguise is what I call em.

Tainted tongues tell you what they think you want to hear to tie up loose ends they tweak

the truth.

Ending every deception with an exception.

Never near by when you need them, but nauseously noticing negative notations on my

life.

Damned if you do, damned if you don't, dogging you behind your back stabbers.

Endless emotions eroding your inner thoughts whenever they enter your presence.

Righteous rivals recall how right this friendship was, but rarely ever reaches out.

Starting silly rumors seeking entertainment so they sideswipe you with cynical sincerity

while they suck away your sanity.

Pretenders...

Resilient

Inspiration already lives inside of me it's like a fire that although at times is extinguished by fear and doubt tends to reignite every time I close my eyes and realize my worth. I am worth a thousand words picture perfect but not perfectly made only made perfectly for that one whose soul dances perfectly to my tempo. Hope is that one thing that beautiful beautiful thing that drives me when I close my eyes I see a sweet peace intertwined with love so deep no longer covering up or hiding behind my pain but embracing it because it symbolizes everything that I have overcame. To overcome is too pick up the pieces dust yourself off and keep fighting and not allow hurt to succumb your very existence. Persistence is something I lack when it comes to displaying affection to someone who holds back I admit it takes me back to a place I dare not face because rejection and neglect parades in that very space. That empty space where loneliness and despair resides so I hide because I know I cannot afford that rent it's too high; because it cost me my self-love my self-esteem and my pride. So instead I love everyone from a distance but I love those who love me back consistently and I won't stop showing you every bit of me the good the bad and the ugly me. The hurt the pain that dwells inside of me that has built and strengthened a better me and has taught me to love you harder and appreciate everyday especially those bad days because if I can get through it I can get through anything.

Unleash this Beast

I'm starting to feel this animal trying to creep up out of me, I'm such a fucking rebel you see, that's why no man could ever handle me, once they get a dose of me, I'm knocking them up off their feet, some think I'm crazy see, but that's just a part of me. No there's no changing me, no rearranging me, look into my eyes and see what has become of me. No more nice and sweet, I'm ready to unleash this BEAST, let my heart and mind roam free, no more controlling me; I'm the one in charge of me. Therefore, I am the only one who can reach in my soul and free, the beast that dwells inside of me.

Why?

Why do I shut down?

Why is it that at times when my face wears a smile my eyes reflect a frown?

Why is it that I pour out love like an art form? Yet my heart feels ripped and torn.

Although I am a woman scorn with each scar, it's like a new woman born.

Why do I blame the world for my pain yet I continuously love strangers without aim?

Why am I carrying around all this emotional baggage when I know I told the last man he could have it?

Why is it that the unforeseen love spirals into messy obscene trials?

Why can't my spunky independence coincide with submitting?

I was once told the first step towards healing was admitting.

So maybe just maybe the why is hidden in me?

Keep on Moving

If you are not looking for someone you can spend the rest of your life with do not even bother looking my way. There is no window-shopping over here, you need to buy the full package or keep on walking. No time for all that smooth talking, these eyes see straight through your lies. I have seen it all and I have heard it all, I have felt the worst pain one can feel and I have cried more tears then you can count. Now save your false hopes & dreams because trust and believe that is something I just don't need. I don't feed off of your shoulda woulda coulda's so keep it moving. There is no point to prove it's settled you either love me hard because hardly lovin won't cut it. And no we can't discuss it, if you have a Mrs. already then why do you need me? No need for deceiving just leave me be.

From the Heart

When a heart is constantly broken into a million pieces, it is difficult for another individual to come in and put all the pieces back together, but for that one who is resilient enough, strong enough and man enough to rebuild and remold that broken heart forever will he have a place near it. There will be many who will try and fail, but when the one has arrived who is destined to help her heart heal, he will know if she receives him with all of her and allows her heart to overflow once again.

FINALY

Poetically I flow futuristically for the world to see and hear me spiritually.

My one goal is to dig deep in my soul and show the world what I hold inside of me.

Dreams and plans to be this woman I see of dignity.

Full of pride with her head held high and her eyes opened wide.

To possibilities and opportunities that I yet see, for you and me of today and tomorrow.

No more sorrow nor pain along with it rain evaporated so we can celebrate it.

A time when we can be free.... FINALY

His Love

Some have it misconstrued; love is not pain but an overwhelming emotion that rains down filling every part of your soul with joy. Love does not toy with your sanity instead; it overcomes you with the sweetest peace of mind one can imagine. Love is not attracted to vanity but it is overtaken by humility's beauty within. Some spend a lifetime trying to find true love's bliss not knowing that they never had to go far just to find a love so truly divine. All it took was to open your eyes and gaze toward the sky and in that very moment, you will begin to realize his love. His love is as calm as a quiet sea with roaring waves of peace. Sweet joy flows like rivers from within my soul pouring out at my feet. I greet my Savior every morning on my knees thanking him for loving me.

Too Nice

Being nice has made my heart cold as ice now thinking twice before I offer up any

advice. Why you ask? It's because

Too nice leads to too many lies and backstabbers trying to deprive me of me.

Too nice leads to too much deceit, friends to turn to foes orchestrating my defeat.

Too nice leads to too many snakes smiling in my face yet willing to do whatever it takes

to take my place.

Too nice leads to too much hate and people busy downplaying my success that they risk

their own fate.

Too nice leads to too many users taking advantage, yeah you know they're borderline

abusers.

Too nice leads to too much confusion, pretending their friendship was genuine were only

an illusion.

So do I continue to be too nice or do I deny God's calling on my life?

I Kissed Her

I kissed a girl and hell yeah I liked it because her lips are enticing and her hips don't lie when she's right here beside me, and we begin hiding in between the sheets making love sweet, surrendering to her curvy physique.

I can't lie as I gaze into those beautiful brown eyes my head is spinning because I am mesmerized. Unspeakable beauty flows from her soul as we start to unfold each other's mysteries. I pull her closer and tell her to relay how bad she has been missing me.

Then we make love for what seems like centuries.

Creating breathtaking memories to share, now the aroma of love fills the air. Good night

Tarnish

I grew up in a volatile household dark family secrets remain untold.

A man I should have looked up to put me through the most, but I would not subdue.

My Aunt told me I was rude, she said your attitude is shity as she repeatedly hit me.

I contemplated suicide multiple times; I thought I would hide behind pills by ending my

life. Back then, when people gazed into these big brown eyes, they didn't see my bright

light. I dropped it low, I even sold my soul anything you can think of I've done, all these

things were an attempt to run away from me. You see I didn't love me enough, yeah I

know my childhood was quite rough and to this day, it's hard for me to trust.

However, I am not ashamed of my tarnished past, because unlike stained glass, my

purpose has been refurbished and my dull shine has now resurfaced.

Our Story

I met a guy it's somewhat hard to describe but his aura took me by surprise.

When I met him I can't lie, I slipped into a trance as I gazed into those green eyes.

Although hesitant, I decided to give this man my time hoping my expression did not

reveal what was really on my mind.

I thought, look at this guy here trying to whisper sweet nothings in my ear, but you know

I'm doubting he's sincere, still I engaged in conversation which later down the line led to

a pretty heavy relationship.

Days turn to weeks, weeks turn to months and I slowly begin to grow impatient.

I yearned for more although I loved him I wondered is this all God has in store.

Eventually we went our separate ways and 10 months turned into days that I prayed to get

back.

Now I am missing him kissing me and treating me like his Nubian Queen.

So instead of giving up on us and trying to love others in such a hurry I'm busy rewriting

our beautiful love story.

Respect My Uniqueness

Just because you don't see the greatness in me doesn't mean it does not exist it simply means your vision doesn't lineup with my eccentric nature.

I will not sacrifice my individuality to stroke your egotistical mindset.

I refuse to be anything other than what I am destined to be.

Perfection escapes me so I embrace my imperfect tempo and dance to my own rhythm.

I love beyond societies limits even though the sting is paralyzing as it flows aimlessly.

I envision you and me walking together sculpting our differences into a beautiful masterpiece.

I admire what makes you stand alone in a crowd of many and still shine, so respect what makes me Me...

Controlling My Own Destiny

Are you working your 9 -5 just to get by the day to day hustle and bustle known as your life? Or are you living?

Every day when your feet meet the floor are you motivated to explore the endless possibilities?

Or is it your reality to allow society to dictate a steady pace on your road to success?

Do you test your limits and push past your limitations? Or do you embark on new ventures with crippling hesitation?

Don't forget that I do understand your frustration, because I too was filled with regret, set with a go with the flow mentality until I opened my eyes to my own realities.

I will no longer allow naysayers to impose on my journey; thinking they really know what's best for me, but only, I can control my destiny.

Autumn

Radiant leaves flow through the autumn skies humming a sweet melody as the wind

awakes from a peaceful slumber.

The beautiful butterfly soars bright and colorful beyond the night in hopes to bring

morning back soon.

In the midst of the moonlit horizon, two lovers fall helplessly and passionately into each

others loving arms.

All the while autumn's love blossoms like sunflowers in the field awaiting the end of a

perfect beginning.

My Heart Cry

My heart is crying out I feel like I'm dying inside all this lying as if everything will be ok.

Its true tears fade away but their stains penetrate my broken heart, leaving scars.

Numbness trickles down my body separating me from everyone who matters; my life

once again is shattered. This never-ending cycle of hopelessness leaves my spirit bruised

and battered. No more excuses because it is useless to blame a man who is just a name to

you, no real connection ties you to roll around with despair. So the moments you share

are based on figments of your imagination, believing fairytales really do come true. My

heart is growing impatient, I'm sick of tear soaked pillows, it's hard to cope when I don't

feel love so my heart tends to spill love and with each drop I slowly feel my soul dying

from within, leaving my heart crying tears of bitterness.

I Found Purpose

A Poetic Journey is a peek into my world, life as I know it no sugar coating, no vision blurred, it defines a survivor.

See the time has arrived when I show the world my pride and joy, two boys blessed from my womb. Life will consume you if you don't know your purpose; life appeared worthless until I birthed it.

First came my king, my first born was a dream come true, although I was clueless of what to do with a gift so precious, God blessed us.

Next up was my little prince charming, born to charm me, his wit is alarming but I wouldn't change a thing about him. So no more doubting, my motivation was conceived when I conceived my own seeds.

Their presence is the fuel I need to feed this ambition growing inside of me. It keeps me alive, my heartbeat. So defeat is never an option, besides I have two men watching, calling mommy. Now fear is behind me, our future is defined intertwined with purpose now it all seems worth it.

I Hate Love

I hate you come on you know who you are forever taking this love shit way too far.

Why do you insist on falling head over heels for an ideal love that'll never be real?

Let's face the music because once again you are dropping everything short of your soul

for a lie it's amusing.

Now you are upset because your heart is abused when you presented it way too easily.

Deceptive images of forever paint your future so vividly and you fall for it every single

time, forgetting about the last time you were left beaten bruised and battered.

Empty promises bombard your laughter, but I refuse because if love is pain then let hate

rain.

Allow it to erase every ounce of pain and repel the penetration of deceit that has so

elegantly disguised itself as a sweet ray of peace.

Bleed

Broken pieces of her soul shattered scattered across the globe as she fearlessly roams the night without a single trace of her dignity in sight. She flags down some random stranger blinded to the dangers she could encounter, then she spends about an hour relieving his erection then off to the next John with no direction just money on her mind and plans to get high. Higher than the moon and she'll return soon to wreak more havoc and support this habit because she has to have it, it helps her escape the reality of her day.

All the while, her five children lay awake and pray that God erase their pain, but her oldest girl feels as though she's praying in vain because her life is in shambles, wondering why mother gambles with her life playing Russian roulette with two bullets. Let's play make-believe and pretend for a second that our lives aren't so hectic and confused, tired of getting abused both physically and mentally; she escapes reality by making her pen bleed so her words feed the nation of fatherless motherless seeds, encouraging them of the light at the end of the tunnel.

No tunnel vision, I envision peace among all and generational curses broken. We can restore wholeness in this Nation all it takes is preparation mixed with a bit of dedication from those who refuse to lose this war on our sons and daughters. No more statistics I'm raising kings, it's what I was sent here for, no more poor me because I'll die to ensure my boys succeed, but until then I'll continue to let this pen bleed...

Just being me (Bubbles)

I am not your everyday run-of-the-mill girl next-door type of chick, no that's not me at all. I have always known there was something different about me that special uniqueness that radiates loudly. I love shouting and reppin what I believe proudly, never mind the consequences. I flirt with second chances and never worry about cheap advances from those who want my body but ignore my soul. I make bold statements with my poetry airing out all my dirty laundry. At any moment, you can catch me singing to a tune that none of my friends would dare listen to, but I still groove. When you catch me breaking out in a dance with no music playing, it's because I am rocking out in my head to my own rhythm. At night, my fantasy world comes to life, I pretend often without thinking twice because it centers me and brings me back to life. I find corny small talk intriguing. Meaningless relationships have a meaningful place next to my heart. The smallest things and simplest places have the most sentiment in my eyes. I thrive on my uncontrollable emotions because they keep me going; always on my toes not knowing the difference between the hopeless romantic and a hopeful dynamic that could be. Some people wonder as outgoing as I appear to be, why do I shut down and shut the world out? Don't trip, It's nothing personal it's just my defense mechanism I keep around for situations when I feel like I'm about to drown in my own overwhelming circumstances. Above all I'm just a fun loving, multi-personality having sweet music loving poet at heart. Yeah I dig art and playing my part is something I've always done so well... until now. Because my rebellious spirit tends to dominate my desire to submit. Contradiction has a habit of slipping from my lips when I begin to speak. So you see what I mean when I say I'm not your everyday run-of-the-mill girl next door type of chick, no that's not me at all.

Secret Admirer

I got a love Jones for a man that barely even knows I exist, but I don't mind because I think about him daily. Those big strong arms, how I fantasize about him wrapping them so tightly around me. Those sexy tattoos from his neck down his chest, boy they do something to me. I stare deep into his eyes when he's not looking, I'm searching for his soul so it'll connect with mine. I long to touch his smooth chocolate skin, and imagine how sweet it would taste mixed with a touch of my caramel tone. I have the slightest clue what it is about this man that drives me so crazy, but I asked him lately does he have a lady? When he asked why do you ask? I shyly replied I'm just curious knowing all the while I want to get to know him on a more serious level. I want to Tango after dark and watch sparks fly. I want to cook him breakfast in bed, and pour his coffee as he dashes off to work in hurry. Fantasies never hurt anyone but I could never act on fickle emotions of lust confused with love. So although I want him so bad I can almost taste his sweet lips next to mine, I'll continue to secretly admire his presence and settle for an amazing friend instead.

Dysfunctional Love

I was in love with you anything you asked I'd do giving up my soul just to be alone with you, forever was the goal you see but your plans were much different. You wanted everything from me except commitment because that role had already been secured by your wife. She saw straight through your lies and knew about me but denied, even after she heard my voice cry out to her she remained right there by your side. You attempted to control my every move who I talked to and what I did on a day to day, popping in to lay your head on my pillow, but you couldn't stay you had to rush back to Georgia to your Georgia peach. You knew you had my heart at your fingertips easily to reach out and pull me near whenever you feared your sweet wife would disappear taking all of her money along with her. It's quite funny you had my mind gone blown away, begging you to stay got old, so you became bold enough to treat me like some ho after you begged for my love. I guess you bit off more than you could chew because when it became time for you to choose you didn't choose me, but you couldn't let me go either. I guess you needed me to fill that empty void of incompleteness. A whole damn year I was you're mistress, it drove me to the point of complete and utter distress, how could I be in love with someone else's love? You made me feel like no other, in my eyes you were more than my lover you were my king; so of course the sting of bitterness was felt when out of love you fell and you pushed me further and further away. Each day I hated you more until that day I showed up at your wife's door, I thought I'd never be free from your web of deceit, but my crazy nature forced you to release me from our bond of dysfunctional love.

The lonely girl blues

Once again I'm hugging my pillow reminiscing about past relationships in hopes that the bitter sweet memories will temporarily erase the painful sting of loneliness.

All the while I am fantasizing about my prince charming, visualizing images of my perfect Mr sweeping me off my feet.

Dreams of my future husband torment my reality as I lay awake gripping my sheets realizing he's just a beautiful figment.

My lonely eyes gaze aimlessly out the window as the moonlight shines lighting up the night.

I inhale exhale calmly to help ease the tension of loneliness that has swelled up in my chest.

I hopelessly await a gentle kiss and a loving touch from my absent lover. I listen to my heartbeat as I lay in the eerie silence of a lonely night.

As I wait I hear my heart harmonizing a tune that makes my soul dance and move to the lonely girl blues.

I Dream

When I dream of you! I dream of a life so different with you in the distance wishing me the best wishes.

I dream of kisses so sweet placed upon my forehead instead of the empty memories we've missed.

I dream of mother daughter dances and second chances when I disobey.

I dream of late night girl talks and playful walks in the park on a beautiful summer day.

I dream of family outings and a girl's day out on shopping sprees.

I dream of Mani Pedi relaxation while I tell you all about my Mr. Right.

I dream of game nights with the grand's and family vacations in the sand.

But most of all I dream of you, only my sweet dreams never came true.

There were no kisses or good luck wishes awaiting me after graduation.

There were no mother daughter dances nor second chances, only glances of motherhood from mothers who stood in.

So I will dedicate to you this open letter to share my heart's desires.

And no matter what our lives may hold, I'll continue to dream of you until my dreams come true.

Crushing on you

Curiosity has me wanting to know you so I'll observe what makes you tick evaluating your core, that thing that makes you distinguished amongst many. In my 29 years I haven't met anyone quite like you, your uniqueness shines through and your beauty radiates complimenting your rugged tone.

I want to figure you out so I'll rifle through your thoughts penetrating your mental and stimulating your physical. You see the crazy thing about it is I haven't desired a woman in years so my fear is what if I can't remember how to love a woman unconditionally. Is this just another phase? I can't quite call it because my head is in a daze thinking about those lips... My God those lips. It's like every single time I get a glance of her my tummy starts to flutter, butterflies fly beneath me and carry me away with my thoughts, slowly flying away to a place where we can act on our desires.

When I close my eyes I want our dreams to emerge, I'll play the leading role and she'll be my costar. We'll travel far in each other's arms learning and growing closer with each obstacle we conquer.

I want to take away your stress and replace it with everything that you're lacking, without you asking. Don't worry it's my pleasure, I'm a treasure no one has discovered, but you see right through me. A diamond in the rough with enough love to last an eternity if only she'd have me.

Daddy issues

Boy do I have daddy issues

Daddy issue number 1 I don't even know him, but I wonder when he closes his eyes at night can he sense me thinking of him.

Does he visualize my eyes crying out for him as I search for his love in others?

Can he hear the frustration in my voice whenever a friend sparks up a casual conversation about absent fathers?

What does he look like?

Do I have his nose? Because when I look at my mother our features don't quite match.

If I knew him would I even like him?

Would he understand my witty personality and the quirks and screws that make me exactly who I am?

Can he feel something is off from a distance and comfort me with his thoughts?

Does he even know I'm daddy's little girl or that I have daddy issues?

If we knew one another would my daddy issues still exist?

Does he love me?

Talk about daddy issues because I love him unconditionally and I don't even know his name.

Thoughts of a Broken Woman

My love life has two personalities Infatuation vs Borderline stalker bitch, I'm sick.

I will love you harder than any person you have ever met, I will pour out my soul at your feet but don't sleep on me because my love is like a drug and if you mix me with that bullshit I will flip the fucking script so quick.

It's funny when I'm not bothering you you're all in my face trying to pull me near, you want me more than a fiend wants crack but once I smack this love all up in your face you begin to act like nah I just wanted a little taste, but fuck that nigga you're stuck once you fuck me nigga you're stuck that's right I said it got damn it.

I'm sick of y'all niggas playing these petty ass games, you're the ventriloquist and my heart's your puppet so fuck it you get what you give.

Now since you give me that bipolar love and run I'm going to unleash the some crazy fun, psycho style.

That bitch so wild is your reaction as I spring into action.

Busting windows and slashing tires and if you're not careful I'll go viral and let the world know how you thought you was going to treat me like some second class hoe, but I showed you.

Bring that ass here boy cause I ain't through I'm sick of you tired ass wannabe players you take these good girls turn them bad just so you can brag to your fellas, now you're dealing with a broken woman and guess what she's coming for you.

A broken woman

A broken woman accepts whatever life throws her way because her bruised heart bare scars that will never heal.

A broken woman cries bitter tears of anguish, she watches in awe as they helplessly spill to the floor.

A broken woman hides behind her pain, it becomes the crutch she embraces as she limps through life shattered in a million pieces.

A broken woman is more content dealing with toxic situation ships then nurturing and building healthy caring relationships.

A broken woman looks in the mirror and sees her worth but ignores it each and every time she settles for second best.

A broken woman requires far too much because she needs to fill the empty void of incompleteness that has succumb her life.

I'm sure nearly everyone thinks that a broken woman will never be able to pick up all the pieces of her broken self and rebuild, but with the right amount of self-love and a determined spirit a broken woman shall reign once more.

Forbidden Fruit

My eyes may see its beauty but they clearly visualize its path of destruction from a mile away. My mind comprehends how poisonous the forbidden fruit would be if I indulged in it, but my heart ignores all signs, optimistic that its nectar would be the binder used to mend it. Why is it that I don't want it unless it's forbidden? The bittersweet taste of the fruit satisfies my appetite temporarily, sadly the problem at hand is the emptiness that is felt after I've fulfilled my desires. It's dressed up just right to entice my love-struck demeanor, so I crave it because it appears to be everything that I'm missing. Unfortunately the morning after isn't so pretty the high has now come crashing down and my lonely heart is exposed. It's clear to see that I'm vulnerable and hungry for love, but I need to be the queen of my own throne not someone else's. I know karma is bound to visit me once I find a love of my own and I won't be surprised if she left behind traces of her presence on my doorstep.

Euphoria

She's delirious over you the love you give her has been way past overdue she wants you, she craves your nature. Kissing your soft lips causes her to slip into a euphoric Trans simultaneously her hands go up gripping the headboard as you explore her body from head to toe. Her head tilted back eyes closed as you separate her knees aiming to please you devour her. Her juices taste so sweet as your cheek presses up against her thigh she belt out a loud sigh that sends a pulsating surge through your body. She can hardly wait until it's your turn because she is yearning to show you everything she's learned. Her scream echoes in the distance as you cause her to realize her sexual peak has been reached. You come up for air and allow her to taste her greatness off your lips then she tightly wraps her legs around you as your hips begin to rotate. Now the roles are reversed and she gets to act out every line that she rehearsed in her fantasy about you. All of the practice must have paid off because your body begins to tremble as her tongue dances inside of you. Now a breathtaking view has been painted in her mind every time she thinks of you. Welcome to Euphoria at its best...

Intellect: A Lost Generation

What is intellect? Is there anyone that can broaden my knowledge of a word that has now manifest from the chest of those who were once denied the opportunity to even read a book? Is it merely afforded to a select few of societies patrons or can anyone partake in this delicacy that has the ability to nourish our minds? I ask these questions out of pure curiosity because I see less of my generation striving for excellence and more pursuing the latest trends like, gold teeth diamond rings and who's on fleek. Nowadays if we addressed our youth and asked what they wish to become as they enter into adulthood they might tell you a rapper or an athlete, now I'm not knocking your God given talent, but is it too much to challenge our youth? If we put more emphasis on education then updating our statuses on Facebook or twitter or posting selfies on Instagram we could exceed our limits. It saddens me to see our little boys and girls slanging and banging, cursing and fighting on camera blinded to the fact that we're inflicting more damage on our race and our culture. As a young child I visualized having the strength of the Rosa Parks or the tenacity of Sojourner Truth, I wanted words to fall off my tongue with such passion and help mold a nation as Maya Angelou did so gracefully. Unfortunately present-day idols are few, young men and women who strive to succeed are labeled with negative connotations; ridiculed because you choose to embrace knowledge instead of walking down a path of stereotypical death is unbecoming of our people. So again I ask what is intellect? It is in fact an obtainable faculty of reasoning and understanding objectively, meaning anyone can have an abundance of knowledge in their grasp, the only requirement is determination. So from this day forward I vow to stimulate my mental capacity in order to remove binding limitations even if that means logging out of

Facebook for a day to indulge in history or turning off my music and picking up a book. I'll do all these things not only for my sake, but mainly for our lost generation. One day I strive to be a positive ray of hope for a little girl with a big mind and a grand array of dreams that she is destined to achieve.

Heaven or Hell

Deep breaths, breathe, breathe, that's all I was thinking

Its pitch black and all I can see is the eyes of a demon

Gunfire, gunfire, left my body leaking and steaming

I hear a voice in my ear, now I'm asking myself am I dreaming

My body getting weaker as the blood enters my lungs

All I hear is the doctor telling me, stay with me son

I'm trying to fight but I can't get this damn demon off my back

I saw a light, so I started to float towards that

Tug of war over my soul, praying hard that God wins

I opened my eyes in ICU and I see that he did

Jayla Nicole

Jayla daddy loves you so much words can't explain, I'd sell my soul for all the things I wish I could change. Should've been there when you were born but I was trapped in the game, but that's my loss, every day I have to live with that pain.

Selfish me, how could I leave your mother hanging like that

She's calling me back-to-back and I'm not calling her back

I felt a pain in my chest that night you were born

I've convinced myself it was stress, but it was my heart being torn

Just knowing I should have been on the side of that bed

Holding your mother's hand as she screamed to the top of her head. Foolish me, foolish me, daddy made some mistakes

I got on my knees one night and asked Lord Show me the way

Ironically I caught 4 bullets the very next day. Baby girl for every sin there's a price you have to pay. I made my bed but I hold my head as I learn the hard way. Could've been dead but my life was spared like that gospel some say.

My sister brought you to see daddy laid up in ICU. I opened my eyes and reached to hold you but I just couldn't move. I started to cry you started to cry then everyone else in the room. Then inside I started to die, like what the fuck am I gonna do?

Lord this can't be true, LORD THIS CAN'T BE TRUE. Baby girl that's when I realized I was living through you. Every time your eyes sparkle, baby mine do too. Every time I feel like giving up I think about my Lil Boo. I fall in love with that smile every time my love comes through.

Yours truly, daddy's baby this is a letter to you…

Lil Fine

I saw this girl around school, but never really thought twice.

When I met her, I swear it was like the beginning of life.

We were both leaving school when she was introduced by a friend.

Intimate conversations lead to lustful sins.

After the first week I'm feeling feelings I've never felt.

Is this that love they speak about, what a card I was dealt!

I remember our first kiss sitting in her car.

As soon as our lips touched it was a stick up for my heart.

She had stolen it and I knew I wasn't getting it back.

It was instant infatuation as a matter of fact.

How could I fall so deep so damn quick?

How could she have the perfect eyes as well as the perfect lips?

How could her voice turn me on to the point where I catch fits?

She's a perfect imperfection wrapped up as a gift.

Despite all of the good, there's always the bad.

I think I took for granted this love that I once had.

I'm not exactly sure, but I don't think she trusted me well.

She called what we had off and it was the beginning of hell.

I played it off like it was nothing, youthful ignorance.

Fate whispers to me sometimes and tells me this was meant.

My life took a turn for the worse and had me thinking it'll never be.

But whether in this life or the next our love is a guarantee.

Every time we converse I'm reassured by faith.

But I fiend for her daily, I don't know how much I can take.

Lil Fine, I need you more than I've ever needed a soul.

You're my love, my inspiration, my motivation, my whole.

Ms. Chocolate lips

I met her about a year ago, unlikely circumstances.

She had lips, like two Twix and the eyes of a romantic.

Chocolate skin, same complexion as those lips.

Instant thoughts of my tongue gliding hip to hip.

All I could think is how one kiss would be a gift.

And once ours met, there was no doubting this is it.

For the first time ever we expressed thoughts about my situation.

Left me with deep vibrations from a deep conversation.

Got me thinking like damn Ms. Chocolate lips could be the one.

Or is this me thirsting for love again however it comes?

Her personality is just as sweet as her kiss.

I've fallen Casualty to Ms. Chocolate lips…

Sleepless nights.

Sleepless nights when will the nightmares end?

Is this life constantly paying for your sins?

Rolling the dice, are they really your friend?

Or are they cold as ice, can you trust that devilish grin?

If I died tonight will I see those heavenly gates?

If I change my life, will the pain go away?

I look in the sky and I pray and I pray.

If I may Lord, I have something real to say.

I take it day by day, but it seems like the stress is taking over.

I try to hide the sorrow because I consider myself a soldier.

Never bend never fold, they don't make them like this.

Secret dreams of being things other people wouldn't get.

Silent screams from deep inside my soulless pit.

Is this as low as it gets, or am I destined for a gift?

Sometimes it seems as if life's a trip because life's a trip…

My Valentine

Could you be that sweet love that many heart's desire?

Could one taste of you set my mind and soul on fire?

You devil of a woman I think you know what you do to me.

Your conversation intoxicates me like five shots of Hennessy.

Damn these devilish thoughts, all these X-rated fantasies.

If you only knew how my mind functions, doubtful you could even handle me.

Even now I'm thinking of feasting on your clit until your juices run down my face.

And looking up at you with a smirk and asking if you want a taste?

Kissing and licking places you wouldn't have thought to think.

Slap you and bite you on your booty until that red ass turns pink.

For the first half hour, no penetration allowed.

Just the exploration of bodies until we've drove each other wild.

And now baby, now it's time for us to connect.

You ride me with a rhythm as I gently sink my teeth into your neck.

We combine lips only so you can taste your sweet taste.

We lock eyes so that I never forget the faces that you make.

Then our orgasms reach peaks that would bring insanity to the mind.

White roses of eternal love for my sweet Valentine.

A Lady Named Hope

I had a dream last night about a lady named hope

We started to reminisce about all the promises she broke

She said she'd never lead me astray but she did it anyway

She said she'd never break my heart our love would never fade away

She looked me dead in my face and sold me all types of dreams

Hypocritical me, I use to tell her the same things

We promised we'd grow together and that would never change

When I was down on my luck I hoped and hoped again

She would show up whenever I least expected

I swear nowadays I'm feeling so neglected

Silly me, I thought hope was perfection

I thought hope was my protection when it seemed all was lost

I thought we had something hope, now you're telling me it's my fault

Until we meet again hope, until we meet again

I'll admire you from a distance, but for now we'll remain friends

My down round

This here is a story about a young lady who deserves the world. You won't meet many like this one, a one-of-a-kind type of girl.

I met her back in high school, she was a friend of a friend. I sat across from her in class. I think that's when the lust began

We began to communicate, but only from time to time. Even though we had others I had no doubt one day she'd be mine.

It wasn't until after high school when the passion really began. The first time I explored her body I didn't want the journey to end

It was instant infatuation, I could tell by both involved. Greedy for what she had to offer. Indeed, I wanted it all.

As time went on what we had grew strong. By my side through whatever, even when I was doing wrong.

Through some of the toughest times of my life, a lot of people left me behind. Had me thinking, like damn, out of sight out of mind.

Not this one, were still friends, this very day. Even though some of the passion that was has faded away.

I didn't really learn to love her until what we had ended. Reminiscing sweet memories from a love I once befriended.

How could I not appreciate a gift as precious as such? How could I not cherish every kiss every touch.

The love she has for my daughter is something I can't explain. A paternal type of love, it's like she went through those labor pains

I admire who she is and everything she's about. Work ethic and growth, the only things that come out her mouth.

How could someone care so much and be so damn kind? How could perfection be so perfect, I swear it rattles my mind?

I could go on forever but everything comes to an end. Everything except the eternal love of my down round, my love, my friend.

Love Gone Wrong

Is this the woman I once loved, something seems so different

She doesn't touch me the same, she doesn't smile, and she doesn't listen

Our love ran deeper than any river ever could

An eternal type of love, inevitable if you would

I used to hold her and caress her mind with my thoughts

When it came to love we showed each other everything we were taught

I use to complement her smile every time I'd see her frown

The sex was magnificent but we'd hold each other for a while

Her kisses made me weak and strong at the same time

Our orgasms reached peaks that would give sight to the blind

We loved stronger and harder than any man or woman ever could

But the vibes I've been getting lately, not so good

Is there another man, could he be stealing my love

Could he be enjoying that smile and the beautiful scent of her hugs

I felt it was time to get to the bottom of this love gone wrong

She promised no deception but I heard the guilt in her tone

Suddenly her eyes watered and her hands covered her face

I could sense the embarrassment but I wanted to hear everything she had to say

Yes she said, there is someone else receiving my love

Yes there's something beautiful that once was us

I hung my head, like damn how could you betray our trust

How could you tell me you love me but hate me so much

She said the blame game doesn't suit you so well

You were the one who broke promises and put me through hell

All I felt was rage, I broke everything in the room

We were supposed to turn the next page, I was supposed to be your groom

She stood up and looked at me with a face so serious

And said love don't live here anymore point-blank period

As a matter of fact my new love is on the way

I just stood there and shook my head without a word to say

I'm thinking of things to do to this person that the sane mind couldn't stomach

Who is this man that stole my love, who is this that's coming

I opened the door and dare I see the face of a woman

www.ingramcontent.com/pod-product-compliance
Lightning Source LLC
Chambersburg PA
CBHW060724030426

42337CB00017B/3008